Comparing Countries

Houses and Homes

Compara países

Casas y hogares

translated into Spanish by María P Coira

Sabrina Crewe

CRABTREE PUBLISHING COMPANY
WWW.CRABTREEBOOKS.COM

CRABTREE
PUBLISHING COMPANY
WWW.CRABTREEBOOKS.COM

Author: Sabrina Crewe

Editorial director: Kathy Middleton

Designer: Keith Williams

Illustrator: Stefan Chabluk

Translator: Maria P. Coira

Proofreader: Melissa Boyce

Production coordinator and prepress: Ken Wright

Print coordinator: Katherine Berti

The publisher would like to thank the following for permission to reproduce their pictures: Ah Fotobox/Shutterstock 11; Akturer/Shutterstock 10; Arterra Picture Library/Alamy Stock Photo 24; Richard Atrero de Guzman/NUR Photo/Getty Images 28; Roman Babakin/Shutterstock front cover (top); Rafael Ben-Ari/Alamy Stock Photo 17; Wojtek Chmielewski/Shutterstock 20; Duncan Cook Drummond/Shutterstock 15 (inset); Jorge Fernandez/Alamy Stock Photo 22; Hennadii Filchakov/Shutterstock 9; Fotokon/Shutterstock 29; Olga Gavrilova/Shutterstock 4; Hkhtthj/Shutterstock 15 (main image); Arne Hodalic/Getty Images 13; Idome/Shutterstock.com front cover (bottom), title page; JTB Photo/UIG/Getty Images 25; Ton Koene/Getty Images 21 (main image); Mark Kolbe/Getty Images 18; Nathapol Kongseang/Shutterstock 21 (inset); Eric Lafforgue/Art in All of Us/Corbis/Getty Images 7; Celia Mannings/Alamy Stock Photo 19; Monkey Business Images/Shutterstock 27; Nikolansfoto/Shutterstock 6; Andrea Pistolesi/Getty Images 16; Pitsch22/Shutterstock 14; J R Ripper/Brazil Photos/LightRocket/Getty Images 26; Friedrich Stark/Alamy Stock Photo 8; George Steinmetz/Corbis/Getty 5; Jimmy Tran/Shutterstock.com 12; Zurijeta/Shutterstock 23.

Library and Archives Canada Cataloguing in Publication

Title: Houses and homes = Casas y hogares / Sabrina Crewe.
Other titles: Casas y hogares
Names: Crewe, Sabrina, author. | Coira, María P., translator.
Description: Series statement: Comparing countries = Compara países | Translated into Spanish by María P. Coira. | Previously published: London: Franklin Watts, 2018. | Includes index. | Text in English and Spanish.
Identifiers: Canadiana (print) 20190199202 | Canadiana (ebook) 20190199210 | ISBN 9780778769422 (hardcover) | ISBN 9780778769637 (softcover) | ISBN 9781427124425 (HTML)
Subjects: LCSH: Dwellings—Juvenile literature.
Classification: LCC GT172 .C74 2020 | DDC j643/.1—dc23

Library of Congress Cataloging-in-Publication Data

Names: Crewe, Sabrina, author. | Crewe, Sabrina. Houses and homes. | Crewe, Sabrina. Houses and homes. Spanish.
Title: Houses and homes = Casa y hogares / Sabrina Crewe.
Other titles: Casa y hogares
Description: New York, New York : Crabtree Publishing Company, 2020. | Series: Comparing countries | Includes index.
Identifiers: LCCN 2019043627 (print) | LCCN 2019043628 (ebook) | ISBN 9780778769422 (hardcover) | ISBN 9780778769637 (paperback) | ISBN 9781427124425 (ebook)
Subjects: LCSH: Dwellings--Juvenile literature. | CYAC: Dwellings.
Classification: LCC GT172 .C74 2020 (print) | LCC GT172 (ebook) | DDC 392.3/6--dc23
LC record available at https://lccn.loc.gov/2019043627
LC ebook record available at https://lccn.loc.gov/2019043628

Crabtree Publishing Company
www.crabtreebooks.com 1-800-387-7650

Published in 2020 by Crabtree Publishing Company

Published in Canada
Crabtree Publishing
616 Welland Avenue
St. Catharines, ON
L2M 5V6

Published in the United States
Crabtree Publishing
PMB 59051
350 Fifth Ave, 59th Floor
New York, NY 10118

Printed in the U.S.A./012020/CG20191115

Contents

Contenido

To read this book in English, follow the purple boxes. To read this book in Spanish, follow the orange boxes. Look for the globe on each page. It shows you where each country is in the world and on which continent.

Para leer este libro en inglés, sigue los recuadros en morado. Para leer este libro en español, sigue los recuadros en anaranjado. Busca el globo terráqueo en cada página. Te muestra dónde está ubicado cada país en el mundo y en qué continente.

Homes around the world

Hogares de todo el mundo

People live in all kinds of places around the world, from forests to deserts. The kind of homes they build depends on the **environment**.

En todo el mundo la gente vive en todo tipo de lugares, desde bosques hasta desiertos. El tipo de hogares que construyen depende del **medio ambiente**.

ITALY

Italy has a rocky coastline. In towns on the coast, people's homes are built close together around the steep cliffs.

ITALIA

Italia tiene una costa rocosa. En los pueblos de la costa, los hogares de la gente están construidos cerca los unos de los otros, alrededor de empinados acantilados.

INDONESIA

Families in the rainforest in Indonesia build houses high up on tree trunks and **stilts**. Their tree houses keep them safe from animals and other dangers.

INDONESIA

En Indonesia, las familias de la selva tropical construyen casas en lo alto de los troncos de los árboles y sobre **postes**. Sus casas en los árboles los mantienen a salvo de animales y otros peligros.

What is a home?

A home is anywhere that people live. It can be a house, an apartment, a tent, or even a boat.

¿Qué es un hogar?

Un hogar es cualquier lugar donde viven las personas. Puede ser una casa, un apartamento, una tienda de campaña o incluso un barco.

Building homes

People can build small homes with their hands. Powerful machines are needed to **construct** buildings in which a lot of people can live.

CHINA

China has a large, fast-growing **population**. People use cranes to build tall apartment buildings made of glass, steel, and concrete.

La construcción de hogares

Las personas pueden construir hogares pequeños con sus propias manos. Se necesitan potentes máquinas para **edificar** los edificios donde viven muchas personas.

CHINA

China tiene una **población** numerosa, de rápido crecimiento. La gente usa grúas para construir altos edificios de apartamentos hechos de vidrio, acero y concreto.

ETHIOPIA

People in Ethiopia use **materials** around them and **traditional** ways to build houses in **rural** areas. They cut sticks to form a frame, tie them together with vines, and then cover them with straw.

ETIOPÍA

La gente de Etiopía usa métodos **tradicionales** y **materiales** locales para construir casas en zonas **rurales**. Cortan palos para formar un armazón, los atan con enredaderas y luego los cubren con paja.

Village houses

Las casas de aldea

In villages, most people live in houses. Houses can look quite different in different parts of the world.

En las aldeas, la mayoría de la gente vive en casas. Las casas pueden tener un aspecto muy differente en distintas partes del mundo.

PAKISTAN

In Pakistan, houses in villages are often built close together. The walls of one house are joined to the next house. People spend a lot of time with their neighbors.

PAKISTÁN

En Pakistán, las casas de aldea a menudo se construyen muy cerca entre sí, las paredes de una casa están unidas a la siguiente. La gente pasa mucho tiempo con sus vecinos.

GERMANY

Houses in villages are often spread out with green spaces around them. Many houses in Germany have **solar panels** to power their homes with **clean energy**.

ALEMANIA

Las casas de aldea a menudo están esparcidas y tienen espacios verdes alrededor. En Alemania, muchas casas tienen **paneles solares** para proporcionar a sus hogares de **energía limpia**.

Clean energy

Clean energy is power created from a source that does not pollute and will never run out. Power created from sunlight or wind are examples of clean energy.

Energía limpia

La energía limpia es energía creada a partir de una fuente que no contamina y nunca se agotará. La energía creada a partir de la luz solar o el viento son ejemplos de energía limpia.

Living in towns and cities

La vida en los pueblos y ciudades

In large towns and cities around the world, more people live in apartment buildings than in houses.

En los pueblos grandes y ciudades de todo el mundo, más gente vive más en apartamentos que en casas.

CUBA

In older cities and towns in Cuba, big houses are often divided into apartments. A lot of families may live in one house, and children often play outside in the street.

CUBA

En las ciudades y pueblos más antiguos de Cuba, las casas grandes a menudo están divididas en apartamentos. Muchas familias pueden vivir en una sola casa, y los niños a menudo juegan en la calle.

FRANCE

City planners in France build modern apartment buildings with families in mind. They design the outside too, with open spaces for playing, sports, and just being outdoors.

FRANCIA

En Francia, los planificadores urbanos construyen modernos edificios de apartamentos teniendo en cuenta a las familias. Diseñan también el exterior, con espacios abiertos para jugar, hacer deporte y simplemente estar al aire libre.

Mountain homes

Many countries around the world have large mountain **ranges**. People who live in the mountains build homes that suit their surroundings.

VIETNAM

In Vietnam, people who live in the hills build houses from wood. Around their homes, they grow rice in **terraced** fields. These fields form steep steps up the mountainside.

Hogares en la montaña

Muchos países de todo el mundo tienen grandes **cadenas** montañosas. La gente que vive en las montañas construye hogares adaptados a su entorno.

VIETNAM

En Vietnam, la gente que vive en las montañas construye sus casas de madera. Alrededor de sus hogares cultivan arroz en campos **en terraza**. Estos campos forman empinados escalones en la ladera de la montaña.

YEMEN

In some areas of Yemen, villages sit on the very tops of mountains. The tall houses are built from stone carved out of the mountain.

YEMEN

En algunas zonas de Yemen, las aldeas están situadas en las cimas de las montañas. Las altas casas están construidas en piedra cortada de la montaña.

Houses by the sea

Casas junto al mar

For thousands of years, people have lived by the sea. The sea provides them with food, work, and sometimes even a place to live.

Durante miles de años, las personas han vivido junto al mar. El mar les proporciona alimento, trabajo y a veces incluso un lugar para vivir.

SCOTLAND

Fishing is an important **industry** in Scotland. Fishing families traditionally built their homes around village **harbors**.

ESCOCIA

La pesca es una **industria** importante en Escocia. Las familias de pescadores tradicionalmente construyen sus casas alrededor de los **puertos** de las aldeas.

Houseboats

Some people live on houseboats on the sea, lakes, rivers, or **canals**.

Casas flotantes

Algunas personas viven en casas flotantes en el mar, lagos, ríos o **canales**.

MALAYSIA

The Bajau people in Malaysia build their houses in the water. They use tin, straw, or wood, and the houses sit high out of the water on poles called stilts.

MALASIA

En Malasia, los bajau construyen sus casas en el agua. Sus casas están hechas de lata, paja o madera y están construidas sobre el agua sostenidas por postes.

On the farm

En la granja

All over the world, families live and work on farms.

Por todo el mundo, las familias viven y trabajan en granjas.

SPAIN

Farms need large areas of land to grow crops. In Spain, farmhouses are often built far from other houses because they have so many fields on all sides.

ESPAÑA

Las granjas necesitan grandes áreas de tierra para los cultivos. En España, las casas de las granjas a menudo se construyen lejos de otras casas porque tienen muchos campos por todos lados.

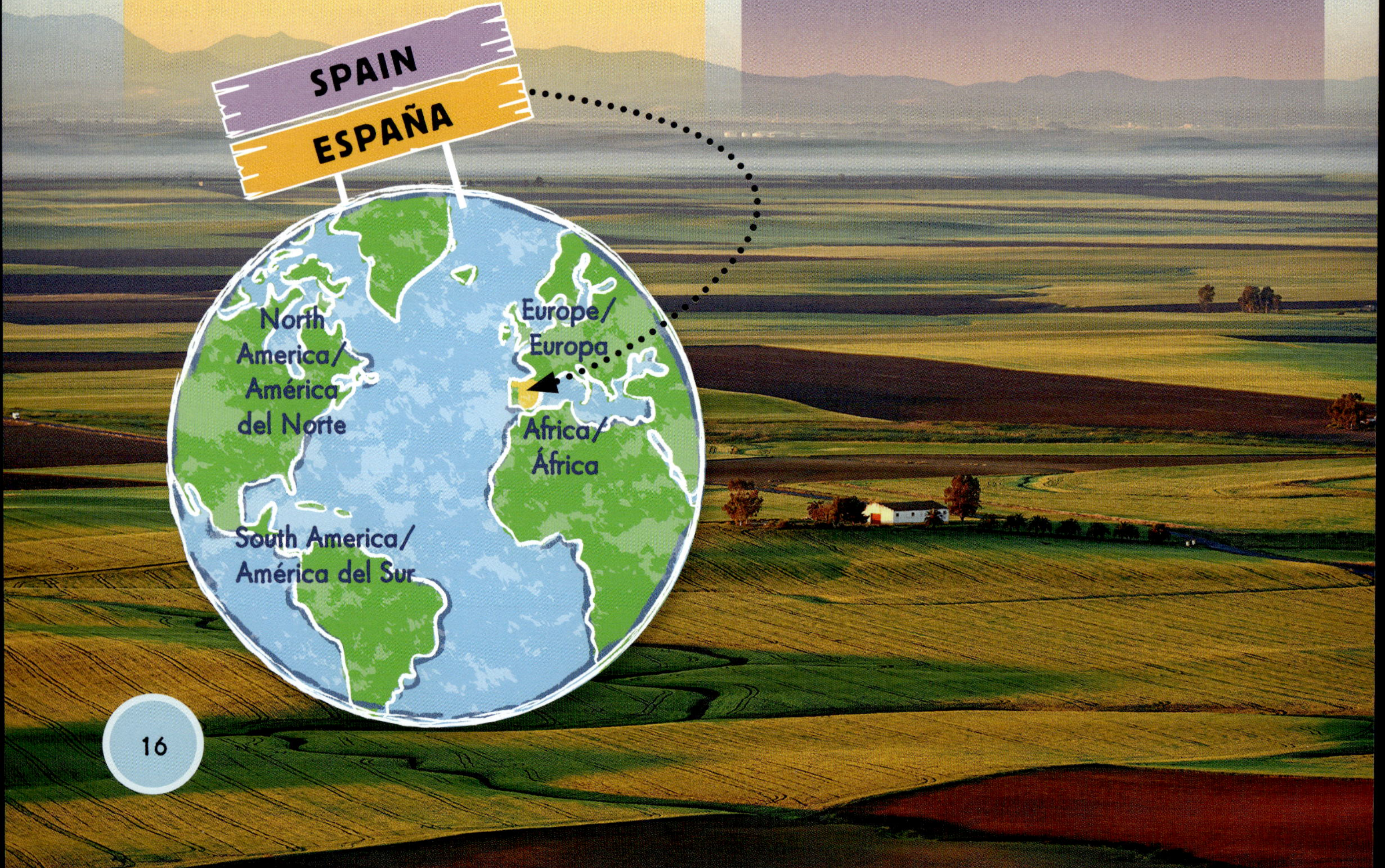

NEW ZEALAND

Most farms in New Zealand raise cattle or sheep. Children who live on farms and **ranches** learn how to take care of animals and do other farm work.

NUEVA ZELANDA

La mayoría de las granjas de Nueva Zelanda crían ganado u ovejas. Los niños que viven en granjas y **ranchos** aprenden a cuidar a los animales y hacer otros trabajos de la granja.

Desert homes

Deserts are dry, hot places. Desert people often build their homes near water. Their homes also need to shelter them from the Sun.

AUSTRALIA

To protect people from the extreme heat, many homes in Coober Pedy, in Australia, are built underground. The rooms are caves carved out of the rock.

Hogares en el desierto

Los desiertos son lugares secos y calurosos. La gente del desierto a menudo construye sus hogares cerca del agua. Sus hogares también necesitan protegerlos del sol.

AUSTRALIA

Muchos hogares de Coober Pedy, en Australia, se construyen bajo la tierra para proteger a la gente del calor extremo. Las habitaciones son cuevas hechas cortando la roca.

TUNISIA

The Berber people in Tunisia are desert **nomads**. They put up their tent homes near **oases**, where they can find water.

TÚNEZ

En Túnez, los bereberes son **nómadas** del desierto. Levantan sus tiendas cerca de los **oasis**, donde pueden encontrar agua.

What is a nomad?

Nomads are people who do not live in one place. They usually travel to follow their herds, and take their homes with them.

¿Qué es un nómada?

Los nómadas son personas que no viven en un solo lugar. Por lo general viajan para seguir a su rebaño, llevando sus hogares consigo.

Living in cold places

La vida en lugares fríos

Many places in the world get very cold in winter. People use different ways to stay warm in their homes.

Muchos lugares del mundo son muy fríos en invierno. La gente usa diferentes maneras de mantenerse abrigados en sus hogares.

ICELAND

Houses and apartment buildings in Reykjavik, Iceland, use **geothermal** heat for hot water, heating, and even electricity. Pipes carry hot water and steam to all the homes in the city.

ISLANDIA

Las casas y edificios de apartamentos en de Reykjavik, Islandia, usan calor **geotérmico** para el agua caliente, la calefacción e incluso la electricidad. Un sistema de tuberías lleva agua caliente y vapor a todos los hogares de la ciudad.

CANADA

Inuit people of Canada's Arctic region traditionally lived in igloos in winter. Today, Inuit usually build igloos to live in when they go away hunting.

CANADÁ

Los inuit de la región del Ártico de Canadá tradicionalmente vivían en iglús en el invierno. Hoy en día, los inuit a menudo construyen iglús para vivir en ellos cuando van de caza.

Igloos

Igloos are made from blocks of packed snow that keep out the cold.

Iglús

Los iglús están hechos de bloques de nieve compacta que no dejan pasar el frío.

Looking inside

Looking inside people's homes can tell us a lot about how families live.

KYRGYZSTAN

Nomads in Kyrgyzstan use rugs and cushions instead of tables, chairs, and beds. They are easy to move with their homes, called **yurts**, when they travel.

Miramos dentro

Mirar dentro de los hogares de las personas puede decirnos mucho sobre cómo viven las familias.

KIRGUISTÁN

Los nómadas de Kirguistán usan alfombras y cojines en vez de mesas, sillas y camas. Son fáciles de transportar con sus hogares, llamados **yurtas**, cuando viajan.

UNITED ARAB EMIRATES

Dubai is the largest city in United Arab Emirates. Many people live in tall buildings that have up to 100 floors. Their apartments have all modern appliances and electronic devices.

EMIRATOS ÁRABES UNIDOS

Dubái es la ciudad más grande de los Emiratos Árabes Unidos. Mucha gente vive en altos edificios de hasta 100 pisos. Sus hogares tienen modernos electrodomésticos y aparatos eléctricos.

What is inside your home?

¿Qué hay dentro de tu casa?

In the kitchen

Most homes around the world have a kitchen. But not all kitchens are the same. How and where people cook can depend on the **climate** they live in.

MADAGASCAR

In hot countries, such as Madagascar, many people have outdoor kitchens. They cook outside in the evening, when the air is cooler.

En la cocina

La mayoría de los hogares de todo el mundo tienen una cocina. Pero no todas las cocinas son iguales. Cómo y dónde cocina la gente puede depender del **clima** en el que viven.

MADAGASCAR

En los países cálidos, como Madagascar, muchas personas tienen cocinas al aire libre. Cocinan afuera al atardecer, cuando el aire es más fresco.

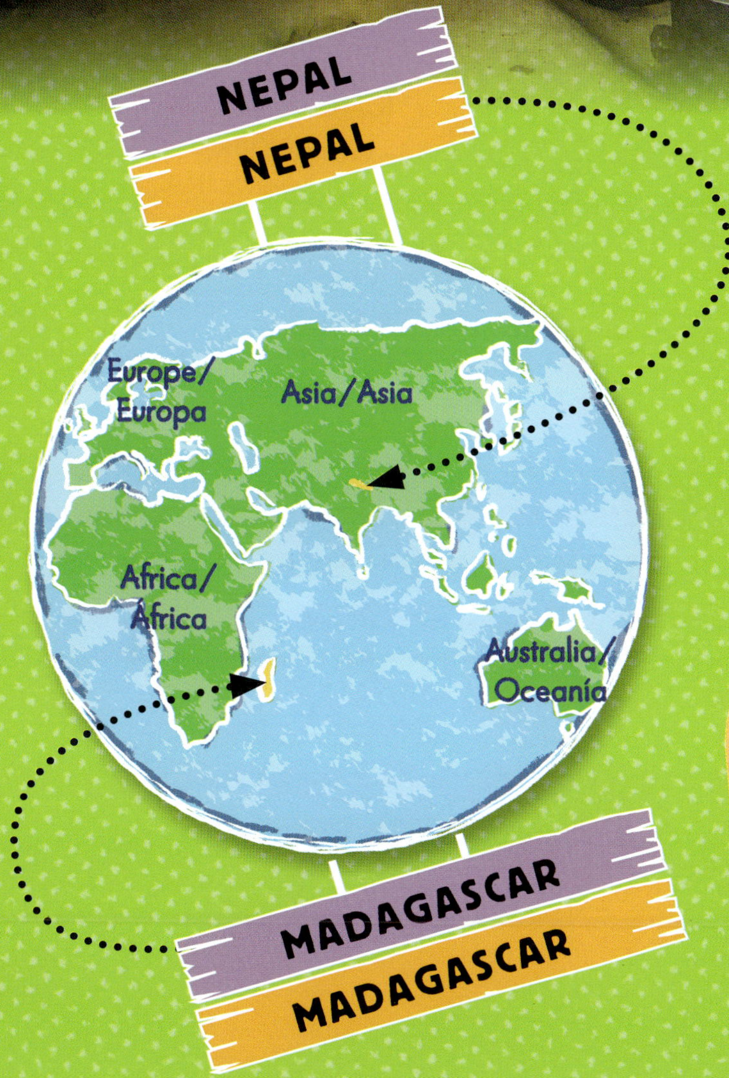

NEPAL

In colder countries, such as Nepal, the kitchen is often where everyone gathers together. The heat of the oven keeps the house and family warm.

NEPAL

En los países más fríos, como Nepal, la cocina es a menudo donde todos se reúnen. El calor del horno mantiene caliente la casa y a abrigada la familia.

Places to sleep

Lugares para dormir

In some places, families spend time and sleep together in one room. In other places, children have their own spaces.

En algunos lugares las familias pasan tiempo y duermen en una misma habitación. En otros lugares, los niños tienen sus propios espacios.

BRAZIL

Much of Brazil has a **tropical** climate where there are many insects. At night, children lie down together under nets. The nets keep them safe from mosquitoes that carry diseases.

BRASIL

Gran parte de Brasil tiene clima **tropical**, donde hay muchos insectos. De noche, los niños se acuestan juntos bajo mosquiteros. Los mosquiteros los mantienen a salvo de mosquitos que transmiten enfermedades.

UNITED STATES

Many homes in the United States are bigger than in most countries. Many children have their own bedrooms with space to do homework, read, and play.

ESTADOS UNIDOS

En los Estados Unidos muchos los hogares son más grandes que en la mayoría de los países. Muchos niños tienen sus propios dormitorios con espacio para hacer las tareas, leer y jugar.

Big houses

The world's biggest houses are in the United States and Australia. They are large, wealthy countries with a lot of space to build.

Casas grandes

Las casas más grandes del mundo están en los Estados Unidos y Australia. Son países grandes y ricos, con mucho espacio para construir.

Amazing houses

The world is full of all kinds of different homes. Some homes are really unusual!

JAPAN

Japan often has **earthquakes**. Some people build small houses in the shape of a dome. This shape is less likely to be damaged by an earthquake.

Hogares increíbles

El mundo está lleno de todo tipo de hogares diferentes. ¡Algunos hogares son realmente inusuales!

JAPÓN

Japón a menudo tiene **terremotos**. Algunas personas construyen pequeñas casas en forma de cúpula. Es menos probable que esta forma se dañe con un terremoto.

What's the most unusual house you have ever seen?

¿Cuál es la casa más inusual que hayas visto jamás?

POLAND

This upside-down house in Poland was built just for fun. You probably couldn't live in one, but they certainly make you look at homes in a different way!

POLONIA

Esta casa boca abajo se construyó en Polonia simplemente pordiversión. Probablemente no podrías viviren una, ¡pero ciertamente te hacen mirar las casas de una manera diferente!

Glossary

appliances Machines that do work in a kitchen, such as dishwashers

canal A straight channel for water, like a river or stream, but made by people

clean energy Power from a source that does not pollute and will not run out

climate The weather patterns and conditions in a region. Tropical is an example of a warm and often wet climate, and a desert has a dry and often hot climate.

construct Build or make

earthquake A sudden movement of rock in Earth's surface that causes everything to shake. The ground can crack and buildings often fall down.

electronic devices Equipment that runs on electricity, such as TVs and computers

environment The world around you or the place you live, including the climate and other conditions

geothermal Using heat coming up from the ground, especially heat from deep inside Earth

harbor A place next to the shore that is safe for boats

industry A type of work or business

material Something used to make other things, such as bricks used to make buildings or fabric used to make clothes

nomad A person who travels instead of living in a fixed spot. Many nomads move their homes when the seasons change.

oasis (plural oases) A source of water in a desert

population The number of people living in a town, village, region, or country

ranch A farm with a lot of land for grazing animals, such as sheep and cattle

range Something that stretches from one place to another, such as a long line of mountains

rural An area with a lot of farms and often far away from a town or city

solar panel A flat object used to make electricity from sunlight

stilt A long pole used to support something, such as the stilts used to keep houses above the ground or water

terraced Built like steps

traditional Always done in the same way and passed on to younger people in a family or community

tropical Located in the region of the world called the tropics, where the climate is warm and often rainy

yurt A round tent covered with heavy material or animal skins used by nomads in Central Asia

Glosario

(appliances) electrodomésticos Máquinas que funcionan en una cocina, como los lavaplatos

(canal) canal Conducto estrecho para el agua, como un río o un arroyo pero hecho por las personas

(clean energy) energía limpia Energía de una fuente que no contamina y que no se desgastará

(climate) clima Las pautas y condiciones meteorológicas de una región. Tropical es un ejemplo de clima cálido y a menudo húmedo, y el desierto tiene un clima seco y a menudo caluroso.

(construct) edificar Construir o hacer

(earthquake) terremoto Movimiento súbito de las rocas de la superficie de la Tierra que hace que todo tiemble. El suelo puede agrietarse y los edificios a menudo se caen.

(electronic devices) aparatos eléctricos Equipo que funciona con electricidad, como los televisores y las computadoras

(environment) medio ambiente El mundo que te rodea o el lugar donde vives, incluidos el clima y otras condiciones

(geothermal) geotérmico Que usa calor que sale del suelo, especialmente el calor de la profundidad de la Tierra

(harbor) puerto Lugar cerca de la orilla que es seguro para los barcos

(industry) industria Tipo de trabajo o negocio

(material) material Algo usado para hacer otras cosas, como ladrillos usados para hacer edificios o tela usada para hacer ropa

(nomad) nómada Persona que viaja en vez de vivir en un sitio fijo. Muchos nómadas trasladan sus hogares cuando cambian las estaciones.

(oasis) oasis Fuente de agua en el desierto

(population) población El número de personas que viven en un pueblo, aldea, región o país

(ranch) rancho Granja que tiene mucha tierra para animales que pastan, como las ovejas y el ganado

(range) cadena Algo que se extiende de un lugar a otro, como una línea larga de montañas

(rural) rural Zona con muchas granjas y a menudo lejos de un pueblo o ciudad

(solar panel) panel solar Objeto plano usado para convertir la luz del sol en electricidad

(stilt) poste Palo largo usado para apoyar algo, como los postes usados para mantener las casas por encima del suelo o del agua

(terraced) en terraza Construido en forma de escalones

(traditional) tradicional Hecho siempre de la misma manera y transmitido a las personas jóvenes de una familia o comunidad

(tropical) tropical Situado en la región del mundo llamada los trópicos, donde el clima es cálido y a menudo lluvioso

(yurt) yurta Tienda de campaña redonda cubierta con material pesado o pieles de animales, usada por los nómadas de Asia Central

Index

Índice

El índice español no sigue el mismo orden que el inglés.